D1429024

Henry II's Great Seal

HENRY II
and Thomas Becket

by JOHN ROBERTS
with illustrations by ROGER HALL

Publishers: Ladybird Books Ltd . Loughborough
© Ladybird Books Ltd 1974
Printed in England

HENRY II

Henry II was one of the three wisest and best monarchs to rule England during the Middle Ages; the other two were Alfred the Great and Edward I. He was also the first King of England to be descended directly from Alfred the Great and William the Conqueror. During his reign, the Normans increasingly thought and acted as Englishmen although, at the court, French was still the language of the King and the nobility. Henry himself could speak no English.

Henry II, first of the Plantagenets, followed Stephen, who had been a brave soldier but a bad king. Stephen's reign is described in the Anglo-Saxon Chronicle as a time when "every powerful man made his castles and held them against the King, and filled the castles with devils and evil men".

The name—Anglo-Saxon Chronicle—sounds as though it might be a modern newspaper, but there were no newspapers anywhere until hundreds of years later. Printing had not been invented and few people could read, other than the monks in the monasteries. It was they who from time to time wrote up the Anglo-Saxon Chronicle, which thus became a sort of national diary. From it we have learned much about how people lived so long ago.

0 7214 0370 0

Henry II was born at Le Mans, a small French town in Anjou. His father Geoffrey Plantagenet, Count of Anjou, had married Matilda, the daughter of Henry I of England. Henry II—then Prince Henry—was their son. When Geoffrey Plantagenet died, the young prince became Count of Anjou; he was also in the direct line of inheritance to the throne of England.

The fact that he was born in France did not mean that he could not become the King of England. Imagine a line, drawn on a map of France, from the coast near Boulogne southwards through Toulouse to the Spanish frontier, with a big loop eastwards towards Lyons. All those parts of France between the line and the sea were ruled by the King of England.

The Plantagenet kings were so called from the Latin name, planta genesta, of the shrub known to us as yellow broom. Geoffrey always wore a sprig of its golden, yellow flowers in his cap. Thus it became a family emblem of the Angevins, as the Plantagenets are often more correctly called because of their descent from the Count of Anjou.

Young Henry grew up to be an adventurous boy who cared more for open-air sports than for book learning. He was a born fighter. He was also fiercely energetic, practical and resolute and had a charm of manner which partly made up for his tough obstinacy.

Henry I had wanted his daughter Matilda, the mother of Prince Henry, to succeed him. The warlike nobles had no wish to see a woman on the throne, and Prince Henry was still very young. So, when Henry I died in 1135, Stephen, his nephew, became King. Stephen had less right to the throne than Prince Henry, who was away in Anjou with his mother. Their absence enabled Stephen to reach London before them. He had another advantage over the young prince: Stephen's brother was the Bishop of Winchester. In those days the powerful support of the Church was very important to a king.

Crowning Stephen, who was really a usurper, was only possible because many of the powerful nobles supported him. They thought that, with him as King, they would have more power. In those days, a nobleman with a strong castle, and a small, private army to defend it, could defy anyone.

The result of all this was civil war in England, and years of misery for simple people whose only wish was to live in peace. Thousands died of hunger or were killed by armed men who robbed them and burned and pillaged their homes. Many were ruined by the illegal taxes and fines levied by the feudal barons; others were forced to work on farms, which had once been their own, without wages or any share in the fruits of their labour.

In the England ruled by King Stephen, the strong dominated the weak; might was right.

Matilda, a granddaughter of William the Conqueror, had inherited his determination and fighting qualities. She was not prepared to sit at home spinning and sewing, whilst her cousin Stephen occupied the throne which should have been hers. Three years after Stephen had made himself King, she crossed from France to join the nobles of the West Country who had grown to mistrust Stephen.

Stephen was defeated and captured by Matilda, and she was crowned in London. But she foolishly released Stephen a year later and civil war again swept the country. After a year of ruinous fighting, Matilda was besieged in Oxford, and narrowly escaped capture. On a snowy night she was lowered from the castle walls wearing a white robe. She made her way through the besieging forces and crossed the frozen river unobserved.

She was hated by the people for her disregard of their misery, and for the ruinous taxation she imposed. It was the lawless barons, no better than brigands, who profited by continuing the war. They changed sides as it suited them, burning and looting wherever they went. Matilda, unable to control them, left the country and never returned.

Though only just twenty years of age, Prince Henry took command and proved his fighting ability at Malmesbury and Wallingford. At a meeting between the young Prince and Stephen, it was agreed that Henry should be the heir to the throne, which of course was his by right.

At the age of twenty-one, Henry came to the throne determined to enforce order and discipline on the unruly barons.

He is described as being squarely built, red faced and with an exceptionally good memory; he made a habit of finding things out for himself. He could work harder and longer than most other people, and it was said of him that he was on his feet from morning till night. He cared nothing for appearances and wasted little time on eating. He had a full-time job to do, and was determined to do it.

In those days of incredibly slow transport, the lands ruled by Henry II must have seemed much more remote from one another than they do today. His lands were his personal possessions, dependent upon him for their government and security. He was the feudal lord of an empire.

From his father he inherited Anjou and Touraine, and as the grandson of Henry I he was the rightful ruler of Normandy and Brittany as well as England. By his marriage with Eleanor of Aquitaine, his lands extended south to the Pyrenees. To look after these areas, he travelled constantly, accompanied by a long convoy of wagons containing the details he needed concerning his various estates. None of his local rulers, whether dukes or barons, knew just when he might suddenly and unexpectedly arrive. Henry made sure he knew everything and neglected nothing.

The Exchequer is now a large government department, and the Chancellor of the Exchequer is a very important person. When Henry I became King, it was already established as a national institution, although the term 'Exchequer' was not then used.

The name originated in Norman times when an exchequer was a table marked out in squares like a chess-board. The money paid to the government was reckoned by means of little counters. The pence were shown by counters placed in the column of squares on the right, the next column showed the shillings and the third column indicated the pounds; other columns were used for greater amounts. The counters were moved up one column and down to the next as the money was added up.

During the reign of Stephen the value of coins could not be relied upon. A great deal of bad money was in use. Some of it had been made falsely out of cheaper metal, and some of the genuine coins had less silver in them than they should have had. This was because it was profitable to clip bits off a silver coin.

Henry changed all this. He suppressed the practice of false coining, and a new coinage was introduced which had a standard purity and weight.

Laws are needed by any group of people living together, whether a small family or a great nation. If everyone did as he liked, normal life would become impossible. Laws are simply rules, and if we do not obey the rules, we find ourselves in trouble. In England, if you were to drive a car on the right-hand side of the road, you would probably not get further than the nearest hospital.

If you were driving a car in France you would find yourself in trouble if you did *not* drive on the right-hand side of the road. In both England and France, if you do not obey the rules of the road, you are a nuisance to other people and a danger to them and yourself.

In your own family, someone, perhaps father or mother, will tell you what you must or must not do. There are rules at school. In the street a policeman might signal to you when to cross over a road junction, and for your own safety you must obey. For your own and other peoples' safety and welfare, you must obey these rules and laws of one sort or another.

Even when people were still living in caves and wearing skins of wild animals, there were things which were 'taboo'—forbidden. Very primitive tribes, like the aboriginees of Australia, or tribes in the jungles of South America, still have taboos. Taboos are also kinds of laws. Often, death is the penalty for those people who do not obey them.

Long before the Romans invaded Britain there were laws; if people did not obey them they were harshly and often brutally punished. William the Conqueror added new laws from France, and his son, Henry I, continued to enforce them. The Norman barons had to build strong castles and keep garrisons of armed men to subdue the conquered Anglo-Saxons. As we have seen during Stephen's reign, this resulted in some barons being strong enough to defy the King.

Henry II was wiser than Stephen. He knew that no law was of use unless everyone obeyed it, whether a powerful baron or a poor peasant. A baron could refuse to obey any law when he was protected by the moat and stone walls of his castle, with bowmen manning the battlements. The obvious solution was to pull down the barons' castles. This Henry proceeded to do, and when the Anglo-Saxon peasants saw that the Norman barons were subject to the law, they were more ready to obey the law themselves.

Disbanding the garrisons maintained by the barons brought problems. Under the feudal system, each nobleman, according to his rank, had to equip and pay a number of bowmen and men-at-arms whenever the King needed to assemble an army. But many of the barons, with no castles to defend, disliked having to enlist and pay soldiers.

So Henry allowed any baron to pay 'scutage' (shield money) instead of providing soldiers.

At certain times of the year, colourful processions of dignified-looking men in ceremonial robes may be seen in some of Britain's principal cities. Traffic is held up by the police to allow Her Majesty's Judges of Assize to pass by. These processions had their origin in the time of Henry II.

The word 'assize', like so many words connected with the law, comes from the French. It means a company of persons gathered together to come to a decision about something. In England today it means a court of law where a jury decides whether an accused person is guilty or not guilty; those who are found guilty are fined or sent to prison by a learned judge.

Before the time of Henry II, accused men who swore that they were innocent were often made to hold a red-hot iron, or were thrown into a lake with their hands tied. If they were not burned, or did not sink, they were declared not guilty. There was also the trial by combat. The accused man had the right to fight the man who accused him; if he won, he was supposed to be innocent. By some oversight this ancient law was not changed until 1818, when an accused man insisted on fighting it out with his opponent.

In the early courts, the jury were occasionally also the witnesses. In those circumstances they could not help being on one side or the other. Today the jury must be made up of persons who know nothing, beforehand, about the case being tried.

Many laws and customs existed before the time of Henry II; it was during his reign that they became organised as the Law of England. This Law has been modified, extended, and occasionally neglected or defied, but many of the legal rights we have today are the result of Henry's courage and foresight.

To be fair to both sides, a jury must be what is called impartial: that is, the members must not be connected in any way with either side. Henry also realised that it was of little use for the jury to be impartial if the judge was not. Before his reign the nobles and barons were the judges in small courts all over the country. A poor peasant had little chance of obtaining justice against a local baron. As the picture opposite shows, he and his family were completely at the baron's mercy.

Henry enforced the system whereby learned judges travelled from London to one court after another in various parts of the country. A judge listened to all the evidence of a case and when a jury of ordinary citizens had given their verdict, the judge awarded the sentence.

The judge was in effect the umpire, and it was absolutely necessary for him to be impartial.

Today it is difficult for us to realise the tremendous power of the Church in Christian Europe during the centuries following the conquest of England by the Normans. Even kings and emperors obeyed a pope.

In those early centuries, the Church had many special rights and privileges. One of them was known as Benefit of Clergy. This meant that no priest could be tried by the ordinary law of the land. It was only natural that the clergy, from the Archbishop and bishops down to the humblest priest, should wish to retain a privilege so much to their advantage.

Sometimes a person who could manage to read only a few lines of the Bible, claimed Benefit of Clergy. This way criminals could escape the punishment they deserved. In the middle of the twelfth century, however, the ordinary people of England had no opportunity of learning to read and write, except by becoming priests or joining some monastic order. There were no books available to them. Printing was unknown in England until Caxton set up a printing press at Westminster more than three hundred years later.

Henry II was determined that England should be governed by one set of laws for everybody, rich or poor, priest or layman. He naturally expected opposition from the Church.

A priest avoids arrest by claiming Benefit of Clergy.

Resistance to Henry II came from a man who was at one time one of his closest friends and, as the King's Chancellor, his most trusted adviser. His name was Thomas Becket.

Gilbert Becket and his wife, the parents of Thomas, were Normans. They had come to London from Rouen and had prospered. In fact Gilbert was at one time portreeve, the Norman equivalent to a mayor of today. As Gilbert Becket was a rich man, his son Thomas was well educated both in London and Paris. At the age of about twenty-four he became a confidential assistant to Theobald, Archbishop of Canterbury, with whom he attended various conferences abroad.

The second of these conferences was held to meet the Pope at Rheims. When King Stephen refused permission for the Archbishop to leave the country, he and his young assistant Thomas Becket, crossed to France secretly in a small boat.

Archbishop Theobald was a priest who liked to be on good terms with whoever was in power. For a time, when Stephen was a prisoner, he had supported Matilda, though later he returned to Stephen's side. However he was secretly against Stephen, and when Henry II was crowned in 1154, the Archbishop was able to help Thomas Becket to a career in the royal favour. Becket was then thirty-five: Henry was in his early twenties. The two men rode and hunted the red deer together in the forests which then covered most of England. They became firm friends.

Thomas Becket was by then a rich man. He is described by a courtier who knew him well as tall, handsome, intelligent and very good company. He proved he was a brave soldier when he accompanied King Henry to Aquitaine, and took part in the popular sport of 'jousting' in which knights in armour fought mock battles. These tournaments, as they were called, were later forbidden by Henry II because they gathered together too many barons and armed knights, with large crowds of their followers. The twelfth century was an age of violence. Men were quick to anger, and we have only to imagine what might happen today if all the members of the crowd at a football match wore swords!

In mediaeval times, a royal favourite was fortunate so long as he remained a favourite! Thomas Becket was given the revenues of abbeys and manors, and when Henry made him an archdeacon of Canterbury he became very rich indeed. It was said of him that "he never dined without earls and barons in his company".

Not many months after becoming an archdeacon, he was appointed by Henry to be Chancellor. It is interesting to read that the Lord Chancellor of England, the most powerful man in the country after the King, had clean straw spread every day in his great dining hall. This was done so that his guests might not soil their clothes if they chose to sit on the floor. Conditions in those days, even in the palace of the King, would seem primitive to us. But when Becket travelled abroad, the people in France were amazed by the riches of the Chancellor of England, with his gold and silver plate and retinue of serving men.

King Henry's plans met with the expected resistance from the Church, but he thought he had a simple way out of the difficulty. This was to appoint his old friend Thomas Becket as Archbishop of Canterbury when Theobald died in 1161.

Becket was the ablest man in England, and Theobald had already suggested that Becket would be the best man to succeed him as Archbishop. Although Becket was an archdeacon he was not a priest of the Church, but there was nothing to prevent his being ordained. So in June, 1162, Thomas Becket, the King's Chancellor, was consecrated as the new Archbishop of Canterbury, having been hastily ordained the day before. Many of the bishops were bitterly opposed to him. They regarded Becket as an intruder.

Becket was in a difficult position. As Chancellor he had helped Henry to limit the power of the Church and to enforce taxation upon its immense revenues. As Archbishop, he felt that he would have to resist the laws he had helped to make, and the taxation he had himself imposed. It is said that he warned the King of what might happen. "I shall lose your friendship", he said, "and you may come to hate me".

To understand what actually happened, we must remember that Henry Plantagenet and Thomas Becket were men of outstanding ability and determination. Hitherto they had worked together for the same things: from then on they were working in opposition to one another.

Becket warns the King that their friendship might end.

The result was as Becket had foreseen, but which his friend King Henry had not.

Previously Becket had lived in great luxury, rivalling that of the King himself. He had countless servants, held lavish banquets, lived in stately residences and enjoyed witty company which revelled far into the night. Suddenly all this changed. He lived the strict life of a holy man, ate simple food and wore a coarse gown.

These were outward and visible signs of a new way of life: what did not show was the change of loyalty. As an honest man Becket had been true to the King whose servant he was: with equal honesty and devotion he was now loyal to the Church. It was the complete change from one extreme to another which amazed Henry. The dramatic consequences of that change have resulted in the many poems and plays and films about Thomas Becket.

As Chancellor, Becket had agreed with Henry and had insisted that the proudest nobleman and the poorest peasant should be equal before the law. Now he fought bitterly and obstinately for the rights of the Church to separate courts for the trial of those able to claim Benefit of Clergy.

Becket enjoying witty company.

Henry resented the claims of the Church, but in a superstitious age he was afraid to defy the Pope. The threat of the Pope's anger was enough to make him call a special conference at Clarendon, near Salisbury, two years after Becket had become Archbishop of Canterbury.

Each side in the dispute made concessions. Becket agreed that crimes against the King's law should be judged in the civil courts, and that only offences against the rules of the Church should qualify for Benefit of Clergy. All appeals were to be to the King from either court, and no member of the King's household might be excommunicated without the King's consent. These, and other very important concessions were agreed by Becket, but before the end of the year he changed his mind.

Warned that his life was no longer safe, and well knowing how ruthless Henry could be, Becket once more crossed to France secretly by night. Possibly he remembered how he and Archbishop Theobald had crossed to Flanders nearly twenty years before, to escape the anger of Stephen.

It was six years before Henry and Becket met again. Becket returned to England, and Henry promised that he should be safe from persecution. Bygones were to be bygones. But neither Henry nor Becket was the sort to forgive and forget. The returning Archbishop was enthusiastically welcomed by the citizens of London and by the monks at Canterbury. The warmth of affection cheered him, although he had little faith in Henry's word. Preaching to the monks in the great cathedral at Canterbury, he said: "In this Church there are martyrs: God will soon increase their number."

Becket returns to London.

Becket's words were to be proved right. Determined still to uphold the power of the Church, he insisted on upholding the sentence of excommunication on the bishops who had defied him. Henry was in France. He had again failed to realise Becket's determination to hold on to what he considered the rights of the Church. Henry was furious. He cried, "Is there none of the knaves eating my bread who will rid me of this turbulent priest!"

Four of the knights in attendance on the King took him at his word, hoping to win his favour. They galloped to the nearest French port, crossed the Channel and made all speed to Canterbury.

Soon Becket lay murdered in the Cathedral, surrounded by the terrified monks. The four sheathed their blood-stained swords, separated and galloped away into the darkness of the December night. They knew that although their sacrilege might serve their King, it would horrify and enrage the citizens of Canterbury.

Whether Henry really desired the death of Becket or not we shall never know. He was a Plantagenet, and Plantagenets were not squeamish about a convenient murder. However, he denied all responsibility when he found that not only the Church, but all the Christian world was revolted by a crime that was brutal as well as outrageous to the Church. His subsequent penance, walking barefoot to the tomb of his former friend, may have been entirely sincere.

Whether Henry was a sincere penitent or not, he certainly realised that the murder of an archbishop in his own cathedral had lowered the high regard in which England had been held by all the Christian and semi-Christian kings and princes of Europe. What was even more serious, the 'turbulent priest' had suddenly become a martyred saint in the eyes of the people of England. Men and women flocked to his tomb: soon miraculous cures of hitherto incurable diseases were reported and believed.

There is no doubt that it was politically necessary for Henry to perform a public act of penitence. The Pope had threatened excommunication and Henry dared not resist him. It was to take him the rest of his life to recover from the consequences of the fateful words he had spoken in anger.

King Henry had enough troubles without adding to them. The attempted conquest of Ireland, on behalf of a brutal ruffian named Dermot, had failed. But Henry had not forgotten that country. In the year after the death of Becket, he had an idea which seemed as promising as that which had made Thomas Becket Archbishop of Canterbury. He would go himself, conquer Ireland, and bring the Irish Church under the domination of the Pope.

Henry thought that the Pope would look with favour upon anyone who brought the whole population of Ireland into the Roman Catholic fold.

Many English monarchs and generals have tried to conquer Ireland. Some have occupied the country by force; none has ever conquered the Irish people. The Romans who occupied and civilised Britain, wisely left Ireland alone.

Henry succeeded in his immediate object. The Pope forgave him, and patiently, step by step, Henry was able to apply some of the laws affecting the Church to which Becket had refused consent. But in return he was obliged to concede to the Clergy their own courts, and their right to appeal to the Pope in disputed cases. The martyred Becket had not died in vain.

The friendship and help of the Pope probably meant more to Henry during the remaining years of his reign than the domestic affairs of the clergy in England. Like all the Plantagenets, he had domestic troubles of his own. The men of this violent and vigorous dynasty were always resentful of any attempted control. They were quick to anger, often cruel in revenge, and always ready to fight, even amongst themselves. Henry later ordered a mural painting at Winchester, showing an eagle attacked by four eaglets representing his four sons, Henry, Richard, Geoffrey and John. One of them was perched ready to peck out the eyes of the parent bird: it was to become only too prophetic.

The Pope forgives Henry.

Henry Plantagenet, at the age of nineteen, married Eleanor of Aquitaine two months after her divorce from King Louis VII of France; he probably had his eyes more on Aquitaine than on a bride eleven years older than himself. According to feudal custom, about half France belonged to Eleanor, and it now came under the control of the future King of England. The marriage was a political one between two ambitious and determined characters.

At the age of fifteen Eleanor had been married to Louis by arrangement with her father, the Duke of Aquitaine. In those days any young princess or daughter of a nobleman could expect to be married for political reasons. These marriages were regarded as alliances, and the bridal pair were allowed very little personal preference. Henry's three daughters were married to the rulers of Saxony, Castille and Sicily; they had no choice in the matter.

The future of his four sons was for Henry a more anxious and more difficult undertaking. Prince Henry, the eldest, had been publicly crowned as the future King of England. The King was determined to ensure the succession: in the absence of Becket, the coronation ceremony was performed by the Archbishop of York.

Gratitude was not a virtue of the Plantagenets. The four young princes were urged on by their mother, Queen Eleanor, to defy the King. The three eldest had been invested with the titles to Normandy, Aquitaine and Brittany respectively, but the overlordship of England and England's King was very far from being to their liking. What they desired was power; power to rule and tax their estates, power to declare war on whom they pleased, power to raise armies and lead them into battle.

Henry considers the future of his four sons.

Henry II cared nothing for the threats of foreign princes. He knew that as a commander he was more than a match for them: as a statesman he was both wiser and equally unscrupulous. In the case of his own sons things were different. He was deeply hurt by their attempts to raise rebellion against him. Prince Henry had gone to the court of Louis of France, his father's bitter enemy. Here it pleased Louis to welcome him as though Henry II were no longer King. When Henry sent envoys to demand Prince Henry's return "*by order of the King of England*", Louis pretended not to understand.

No doubt Louis thought it was amusing to tell the envoys that the King of England, indicating Prince Henry, was his honoured guest, and that King Henry II was only the ex-King. Richard and Geoffrey seized the opportunity of annoying their father by hurrying to join Prince Henry. King Louis was very willing to receive them. The four of them probably found it very entertaining to picture the anger of their royal father.

They found it much less amusing when Henry reacted swiftly by crossing to France and defeating a rebellious army in Brittany. The King of France considered it prudent to think again. An angry King Henry in England was a long way away: a victorious King Henry in France with what seemed an invincible army was much too near for comfort.

Somewhat unconvincingly, Louis had promised to help Prince Henry and his two brothers. In return they had to swear not to make peace with their father without Louis' consent. He now decided that it would perhaps be wiser not to wait to be asked.

King Louis and Prince Henry ignore the envoys of Henry II.

In the feudal days of the twelfth century, the question of who paid homage to whom was very important. Men thought of a sort of human pyramid, with everybody owing allegiance to someone immediately above him. The King was at the apex and naturally the simple peasant was at the bottom. The paying of homage simply meant that a baron who held estates in the area of a duke was required to swear to serve the duke in peace or war.

When Henry divided various areas and estates in France between his sons, the question of homage became involved. Geoffrey had refused to pay homage as Count of Brittany to his elder brother Henry, his overlord.

Geoffrey and Richard had now allied themselves with Prince Henry, and a sort of peace was patched up. None of these three typical Plantagenets had any intention of keeping the peace if he saw an opportunity of successfully making trouble for his father. When Richard invaded Normandy, which he claimed should be his by right, King Henry proved that he was too strong for him. Richard submitted and was forgiven.

Henry's forgiveness came almost to be taken for granted by his ungrateful sons. One after another they had sworn homage to him, only to rebel again when it suited them. On one occasion Geoffrey invited his father to a conference at Limoges. Although Henry had been warned against going, his wish to live at peace with all his sons made him disregard the warning. As he rode up to the fortified gateway of the town, he was met by a shower of arrows from the battlements. The warning had been fully justified.

No father ever forgave his sons so frequently and had so little gratitude. Affection was not enough. All four of them were as greedy as they were dishonest, as unscrupulous as they were violent. Their solemn promises were worthless unless it was to their advantage to keep them: their friendship was more dangerous than their open hostility.

Being themselves untrustworthy, they trusted no-one. Each knew that to enter the castle of another brother was to accept a risk. That was why they preferred to meet in the open air. Halfway between Paris and Dieppe there was a famous tree, the ancient Elm of Gisors. Under its spreading branches conferences could be conducted in comparative safety. Even this precaution was no guarantee against the violent lawlessness of the times. When King Henry and some French envoys met on a summer's day, instead of making peace, they began to fight about which of them should sit in the shade.

Prince Henry died of fever in France before he was thirty, and three years later, in 1186, Geoffrey was unhorsed at a tournament and trampled to death. Prince Richard was now heir to the throne. King Henry was worn out by his unceasing efforts for the improvement of his country, and the treachery and ingratitude of his sons. Prince John, the youngest and best loved of his sons was twenty-two when Richard again took up arms against his long-suffering father.

Henry was in France in command of an army in 1189. Again he was prepared to make peace and forgive Richard, but in a violent thunderstorm he was struck by lightning. Shaken and almost unconscious, he was carried to the Castle of Chinon.

Later, when the King was given the list of those who had been concerned in this final rebellion of an unworthy son, his last illusion was shattered. At the head of the list was the name of Prince John.

Already a sick man, Henry lost all desire to live. When Richard came to ask forgiveness for the last time, Henry refused to speak to him. He died soon afterwards.

Henry Plantagenet, King of England, reigned for thirty-five of the most important years in the history of Norman England. Previously, under Stephen, the gangs of criminals maintained by the local barons burned and looted as they pleased. Villagers who saw a few horse-men riding towards their homes, fled in dismay. Travellers on the wretched roads went in fear of their lives. For years England was a waste of burnt-out farms and townships. By demolishing eleven hundred castles, Henry brought hope of better times; and by his wise government a man was enabled to claim his just rights. It is difficult to imagine what this meant to a peasant whose father and grandfather had never known what it was to live safely from day to day.

Under the three following monarchs, Richard, John and Henry III, the people looked back to the good times of Henry II. Not until more than eighty years after Henry's death was there again in England a government with similar safeguards for the freedom of the individual.

A Ladybird Book
Series 561